J R HARRIS

Health Insurance Hacks

Unlock Financial Stability

Copyright © 2024 by J R HARRIS

All rights reserved. No part of this publication may be reproduced, stored or transmitted in any form or by any means, electronic, mechanical, photocopying, recording, scanning, or otherwise without written permission from the publisher. It is illegal to copy this book, post it to a website, or distribute it by any other means without permission.

J R HARRIS asserts the moral right to be identified as the author of this work.

J R HARRIS has no responsibility for the persistence or accuracy of URLs for external or third-party Internet Websites referred to in this publication and does not guarantee that any content on such Websites is, or will remain, accurate or appropriate.

Designations used by companies to distinguish their products are often claimed as trademarks. All brand names and product names used in this book and on its cover are trade names, service marks, trademarks and registered trademarks of their respective owners. The publishers and the book are not associated with any product or vendor mentioned in this book. None of the companies referenced within the book have endorsed the book.

First edition

This book was professionally typeset on Reedsy.
Find out more at reedsy.com

Contents

Chapter 1	**1**
Health Insurance Hacks: Unlock Financial Stability	1
Introduction	2
Introduction	2
Chapter 1: Understanding Health Insurance	3
What is Health Insurance?	3
Why Health Insurance is Important	3
How Health Insurance Works	4
Types of Health Insurance Plans	4
Employer-Sponsored Insurance	4
Individual and Family Plans	4
Government Programs	5
Key Terms to Know	5
How to Read an Insurance Policy	6
Understanding Insurance Networks	6
Examples of Understanding Health Insurance	7
Example 1: Choosing a Plan Based on Needs	7
Example 2: Maximizing Preventive Care	8
Useful Websites	8
Chapter 2: Choosing the Right Health Insurance Plan	10
Assessing Your Needs	10
Comparing Plans	11
Premiums	11

Deductibles	11
Copayments and Coinsurance	11
Out-of-Pocket Maximum	12
Understanding Networks	12
In-Network Providers	12
Out-of-Network Providers	13
Types of Networks	13
Evaluating Plan Benefits	13
Preventive Care	14
Prescription Drug Coverage	14
Specialist and Mental Health Services	14
Additional Benefits	14
Examples	15
Example 1: Choosing a Plan Based on Needs	15
Example 2: Balancing Premiums and Deductibles	15
Example 3: Ensuring Comprehensive Coverage	15
Useful Websites	16
Chapter 3: Maximizing Your Health Insurance Benefits	17
Preventive Care	17
Importance of Preventive Care	17
Examples of Preventive Services	18
How to Use Preventive Services	18
Using In-Network Providers	18
Benefits of In-Network Providers	19
Finding In-Network Providers	19
Understanding and Using Telehealth	19
Benefits of Telehealth	19
Examples of Telehealth Services	20
How to Use Telehealth	20
Managing Medications	20

Understanding Your Plan's Formulary	21
Cost-Saving Strategies for Medications	21
Examples of Managing Medications	21
Understanding Additional Plan Features	22
Wellness Programs	22
Employee Assistance Programs (EAPs)	22
Health Coaching	23
Examples of Additional Plan Features	23
Useful Websites	23
Chapter 4: Financial Strategies for Health Insurance	25
Health Savings Accounts (HSAs)	25
Benefits of HSAs	25
How to Use an HSA	26
Example	26
Flexible Spending Accounts (FSAs)	27
Benefits of FSAs	27
Limitations of FSAs	27
How to Use an FSA	27
Example	28
Tax Deductions and Credits	28
Self-Employed Health Insurance Deduction	28
Itemized Deductions for Medical Expenses	28
Health Coverage Tax Credit (HCTC)	29
Example	29
Reducing Healthcare Costs Through Financial Strategies	29
Shopping for Services	29
Using Preventive Services	30
Example	30
Utilizing Employer Benefits	30
Wellness Programs	30

Employee Assistance Programs (EAPs)	31
Example	31
Useful Websites	31
Chapter 5: Reducing Healthcare Costs	33
Shopping for Services	33
Price Transparency Tools	33
Example	34
Negotiating Medical Bills	34
Steps to Negotiate Medical Bills	34
Example	35
Understanding Medical Billing Errors	35
Common Medical Billing Errors	35
Steps to Address Billing Errors	36
Example	36
Utilizing Cost-Saving Resources	36
Prescription Discount Programs	37
Community Health Clinics	37
Financial Assistance Programs	37
Examples of Cost-Saving Resources	37
Example 1: Prescription Discount Program	38
Example 2: Community Health Clinic	38
Example 3: Financial Assistance Program	38
Useful Websites	38
Chapter 6: Legal Considerations	40
Knowing Your Rights Under the Affordable Care Act (ACA)	40
Key Provisions of the ACA	40
Example	41
Appeals and Grievances	41
Steps to Appeal a Denied Claim	42
Example	42

Filing Grievances	42
Steps to File a Grievance	43
Example	43
Understanding COBRA	43
Key Aspects of COBRA	44
How to Enroll in COBRA	44
Example	44
Legal Protections for Health Insurance Consumers	45
Health Insurance Portability and Accountability Act (HIPAA)	45
Mental Health Parity and Addiction Equity Act (MHPAEA)	45
Example	46
Useful Websites	46
Chapter 7: Long-Term Planning and Health Insurance	48
Insurance and Retirement	48
Medicare	48
Medigap (Medicare Supplement Insurance)	49
Retirement Health Insurance Strategies	49
Example	50
Planning for Long-Term Care	50
Long-Term Care Insurance	50
Self-Funding Long-Term Care	51
Example	51
Estate Planning and Health Insurance	52
Health Care Directives	52
Financial Power of Attorney	52
Trusts	52
Example	53
Resources for Long-Term Planning	53
Chapter 8: Leveraging Technology for Health Insurance...	55

Health Insurance Portals and Mobile Apps	55
Features of Health Insurance Portals and Apps	55
Example	56
Personal Health Records (PHRs)	56
Benefits of PHRs	56
Popular PHR Platforms	57
Example	57
Telehealth and Virtual Care	57
Advantages of Telehealth	58
Types of Telehealth Services	58
Example	58
Health and Fitness Apps	58
Popular Health and Fitness Apps	59
Integrating Apps with Health Insurance	59
Example	59
Wearable Technology	59
Benefits of Wearable Technology	60
Example	60
Online Health Communities	60
Benefits of Online Health Communities	60
Popular Online Health Communities	61
Example	61
Useful Websites and Apps	61
Conclusion	63
Conclusion	63
Resources	63

Chapter 1

Health Insurance Hacks: Unlock Financial Stability

Introduction

Introduction

Financial stability is a goal many strive for, and health insurance can be a key component in achieving it. This book will guide you through understanding health insurance, maximizing its benefits, and incorporating it into your broader financial plan. By the end of this book, you'll have a solid foundation for using health insurance to support your financial stability.

Chapter 1: Understanding Health Insurance

What is Health Insurance?

Health insurance is a contract between you and an insurance company, where you pay regular premiums in exchange for coverage of a portion of your healthcare costs. This arrangement helps protect you from the high costs associated with medical care. The insurer negotiates rates with healthcare providers, ensuring you get services at lower costs than you would pay out of pocket.

Why Health Insurance is Important

Health insurance plays a critical role in managing your financial risk. Without insurance, medical expenses can be overwhelming and lead to significant debt. Health insurance not only provides financial protection but also grants access to a network of healthcare providers and preventive services that can help you maintain your health and avoid costly medical issues in the future.

How Health Insurance Works

When you have health insurance, you pay a premium to maintain coverage. When you need medical care, your insurance helps cover the costs according to the terms of your policy. Typically, you'll also pay some out-of-pocket expenses, such as copayments, deductibles, and coinsurance, before your insurance kicks in.

Types of Health Insurance Plans

Health insurance comes in several forms, each with its own features, benefits, and costs. Understanding these types can help you choose the best plan for your needs.

Employer-Sponsored Insurance

- **Overview**: Provided by employers, these plans often cover employees and their dependents.
- **Benefits**: Lower premiums due to employer contributions, access to group rates, and comprehensive coverage options.
- **Examples**: Large companies like Google and Amazon offer extensive health benefits, including medical, dental, and vision coverage.

Individual and Family Plans

- **Overview**: Purchased directly from insurance companies or through health insurance marketplaces.
- **Benefits**: Flexibility to choose plans that best meet your needs, options for different coverage levels and networks.

- **Examples**: A self-employed graphic designer may purchase an individual plan through Healthcare.gov to cover her and her family.

Government Programs

- **Medicare**: Federal program for people aged 65 and older, and certain younger individuals with disabilities.
- **Medicaid**: State and federal program providing coverage for low-income individuals and families.
- **Children's Health Insurance Program (CHIP)**: Offers low-cost coverage to children in families that earn too much to qualify for Medicaid.
- **Examples**: A senior citizen might enroll in Medicare Part A for hospital insurance and Part B for medical insurance. A low-income family might use Medicaid for comprehensive healthcare coverage.

Key Terms to Know

Understanding key health insurance terms can help you navigate your plan and make informed decisions about your care.

- **Premium**: The amount you pay for your health insurance every month or year.
- **Deductible**: The amount you must pay out-of-pocket for healthcare services before your insurance begins to pay.
- **Copayment (Copay)**: A fixed amount you pay for a covered healthcare service, typically at the time of service.
- **Coinsurance**: Your share of the costs of a covered service, calculated as a percentage of the allowed amount for the

service.
- **Out-of-Pocket Maximum**: The most you'll pay during a policy period (usually a year) before your insurance covers 100% of the allowed amount.

How to Read an Insurance Policy

Understanding your insurance policy is crucial to making the most of your coverage. Here's how to decode the essential parts:

1. **Summary of Benefits and Coverage (SBC)**: Provides a snapshot of what the plan covers, including costs for common medical services.
2. **Policy Documents**: Detailed descriptions of coverage, exclusions, and limits. It includes information about premiums, deductibles, copayments, coinsurance, and out-of-pocket maximums.
3. **Provider Network**: Lists in-network providers and facilities. Staying within this network can save you money.
4. **Prescription Drug Coverage**: Details on the formulary, which is a list of covered medications, including tiers that affect your copay or coinsurance amounts.

Understanding Insurance Networks

Insurance networks are groups of healthcare providers that have agreed to provide services to plan members at discounted rates. Networks can vary widely between plans.

- **In-Network Providers**: Healthcare providers who have contracted with your insurance plan to offer services at ne-

gotiated rates. Using in-network providers usually results in lower out-of-pocket costs.
- **Out-of-Network Providers**: Providers who have not contracted with your insurance plan. Visiting out-of-network providers typically results in higher costs and sometimes no coverage at all.
- **Network Types**:
- **Health Maintenance Organization (HMO)**: Requires you to choose a primary care physician (PCP) and get referrals to see specialists. Coverage is typically limited to in-network providers.
- **Preferred Provider Organization (PPO)**: Offers more flexibility in choosing healthcare providers and does not require referrals to see specialists. Out-of-network care is covered but at a higher cost.
- **Exclusive Provider Organization (EPO)**: Combines features of HMOs and PPOs, requiring you to use in-network providers but without the need for referrals.
- **Point of Service (POS)**: Requires a primary care physician and referrals, but allows for out-of-network care at higher costs.

Examples of Understanding Health Insurance

Example 1: Choosing a Plan Based on Needs

Maria, a 28-year-old freelance writer, needs a plan that covers her regular doctor visits and prescriptions for asthma. She compares different individual plans on Healthcare.gov, focusing on those with lower copayments for office visits and medications. She chooses a silver plan with moderate premiums and a reasonable out-of-pocket maximum, ensuring she can manage her healthcare expenses without breaking the bank.

Example 2: Maximizing Preventive Care

Tom, a 45-year-old software engineer with employer-sponsored insurance, takes full advantage of the preventive services covered by his plan. He schedules annual physicals, cholesterol screenings, and flu shots at no additional cost. By doing so, he maintains his health and catches potential issues early, avoiding more expensive treatments down the line.

Useful Websites

- Healthcare.gov: Official health insurance marketplace for individual and family plans.
- Medicare.gov: Official site for Medicare information.
- Medicaid.gov: Information on Medicaid and CHIP programs.
- NerdWallet Health Insurance Guide: Comprehensive guide to understanding and choosing health insurance.

By understanding the basics of health insurance, the different types of plans available, and key terms, you can make informed decisions that support your financial stability. The following chapters will delve deeper into choosing the right plan, maximizing benefits, and integrating health insurance into your broader financial strategy.

CHAPTER 1: UNDERSTANDING HEALTH INSURANCE

Chapter 2: Choosing the Right Health Insurance Plan

Selecting the right health insurance plan is a crucial step in managing your healthcare costs and ensuring you receive the necessary medical care. This chapter will guide you through assessing your healthcare needs, comparing different plans, understanding insurance networks, and evaluating plan benefits.

Assessing Your Needs

Before diving into the details of various health insurance plans, take a moment to assess your healthcare needs. Consider the following factors for yourself and your dependents:

1. **Medical History**: Review your past medical history, including chronic conditions, surgeries, and regular medications.
2. **Frequency of Doctor Visits**: Estimate how often you visit healthcare providers for routine check-ups, specialist consultations, and urgent care.
3. **Medications**: List any prescription drugs you or your family members take regularly.
4. **Planned Procedures**: Consider any upcoming medical procedures, such as surgeries or treatments.

CHAPTER 2: CHOOSING THE RIGHT HEALTH INSURANCE PLAN

5. **Family Needs**: Assess the healthcare needs of your spouse, children, or other dependents who will be covered under your plan.

Comparing Plans

Once you have a clear understanding of your healthcare needs, it's time to compare different health insurance plans. Here are the key factors to consider:

Premiums

- **Definition**: The monthly or annual amount you pay for your health insurance.
- **Considerations**: Higher premiums often mean lower out-of-pocket costs and vice versa. Balance the premium with your ability to pay and expected healthcare usage.

Deductibles

- **Definition**: The amount you pay out-of-pocket before your insurance starts covering costs.
- **Considerations**: Higher deductibles usually result in lower premiums. If you anticipate frequent healthcare usage, a lower deductible may be more cost-effective.

Copayments and Coinsurance

- **Copayments**: Fixed fees you pay for specific services, such as doctor visits or prescriptions.
- **Coinsurance**: Your share of the cost of a covered service,

expressed as a percentage.
- **Considerations**: Lower copayments and coinsurance rates can reduce your out-of-pocket expenses for regular medical care.

Out-of-Pocket Maximum

- **Definition**: The maximum amount you'll pay in a policy period before your insurance covers 100% of the allowed amount.
- **Considerations**: Plans with lower out-of-pocket maximums can protect you from excessive medical expenses in the event of serious illness or injury.

Understanding Networks

Health insurance plans have different network structures, affecting which healthcare providers you can see and how much you'll pay for services. Understanding these networks is essential in choosing the right plan.

In-Network Providers

- **Definition**: Healthcare providers who have contracted with your insurance plan to offer services at negotiated rates.
- **Benefits**: Lower out-of-pocket costs, better coordination of care, and streamlined claims processing.

Out-of-Network Providers

- **Definition**: Providers who have not contracted with your insurance plan.
- **Drawbacks**: Higher costs, potential lack of coverage, and more complex claims processing.

Types of Networks

- **Health Maintenance Organization (HMO)**: Requires you to choose a primary care physician (PCP) and get referrals to see specialists. Coverage is limited to in-network providers, except in emergencies.
- **Preferred Provider Organization (PPO)**: Offers more flexibility in choosing healthcare providers and does not require referrals to see specialists. Out-of-network care is covered but at a higher cost.
- **Exclusive Provider Organization (EPO)**: Combines features of HMOs and PPOs, requiring you to use in-network providers but without the need for referrals.
- **Point of Service (POS)**: Requires a primary care physician and referrals, but allows for out-of-network care at higher costs.

Evaluating Plan Benefits

Beyond the basic costs and network structures, it's important to evaluate the specific benefits each plan offers. Consider the following:

Preventive Care

- **Importance**: Many plans cover preventive services, such as immunizations, screenings, and annual check-ups, at no additional cost.
- **Evaluation**: Ensure the plan covers the preventive care services you and your family need.

Prescription Drug Coverage

- **Formulary**: A list of medications covered by the plan. Check if your regular prescriptions are included and at what cost.
- **Tiers**: Understand the tier structure of the formulary, as different tiers may have varying copayments or coinsurance rates.

Specialist and Mental Health Services

- **Specialists**: If you require specialist care, ensure the plan covers these services and includes your preferred providers.
- **Mental Health**: Mental health coverage is essential. Confirm that the plan offers comprehensive mental health and substance abuse services.

Additional Benefits

- **Dental and Vision**: Some plans offer dental and vision coverage or allow you to purchase additional coverage.
- **Telehealth**: Check if the plan includes telehealth services, which can provide convenient and cost-effective healthcare options.

- **Wellness Programs**: Some plans offer wellness programs, such as gym memberships, smoking cessation programs, or weight loss support.

Examples

Example 1: Choosing a Plan Based on Needs

Maria, a 28-year-old freelance writer, needs a plan that covers her regular doctor visits and prescriptions for asthma. She compares different individual plans on Healthcare.gov, focusing on those with lower copayments for office visits and medications. She chooses a silver plan with moderate premiums and a reasonable out-of-pocket maximum, ensuring she can manage her healthcare expenses without breaking the bank.

Example 2: Balancing Premiums and Deductibles

Tom, a 45-year-old software engineer, is generally healthy but wants to be prepared for unexpected medical expenses. He compares several plans offered by his employer and decides on a high-deductible health plan (HDHP) with a health savings account (HSA). This plan has lower premiums, and the HSA allows him to save money tax-free for future medical expenses.

Example 3: Ensuring Comprehensive Coverage

Lisa, a 50-year-old with a history of heart disease, needs comprehensive coverage that includes regular visits to a cardiologist and prescription medications. She evaluates plans on her state's health insurance marketplace and selects a gold plan with higher premiums but lower copayments and out-of-pocket maximums. This plan ensures she can afford her regular specialist visits and medications without financial strain.

Useful Websites

- Healthcare.gov Plan Finder: Compare health insurance plans.
- NerdWallet Health Insurance Comparison: Tools and tips for comparing health insurance plans.
- HealthInsurance.org: Information on health insurance options and state-specific resources.
- Kaiser Family Foundation (KFF): In-depth research and analysis on health insurance and healthcare issues.

By carefully assessing your healthcare needs, comparing different plans, understanding network structures, and evaluating specific benefits, you can choose a health insurance plan that provides the coverage you need at a cost you can afford. The right plan will not only protect your health but also support your financial stability.

Chapter 3: Maximizing Your Health Insurance Benefits

Maximizing your health insurance benefits can significantly reduce your healthcare costs and enhance your overall health. This chapter will guide you through preventive care, using in-network providers, leveraging telehealth, managing medications, and understanding additional plan features.

Preventive Care

Preventive care is essential for maintaining good health and catching potential issues early. Most insurance plans cover preventive services at no additional cost to you. These services include annual check-ups, vaccinations, and screenings.

Importance of Preventive Care

- **Early Detection**: Regular screenings and check-ups can detect health issues before they become severe, allowing for early intervention.
- **Cost Savings**: Preventive care can prevent expensive treatments down the road. For example, managing high blood pressure with regular check-ups and medication can pre-

vent costly heart disease.
- **Improved Health**: Staying on top of preventive care can improve your overall health and well-being.

Examples of Preventive Services

- **Annual Physicals**: Routine check-ups with your primary care physician.
- **Immunizations**: Vaccines for flu, pneumonia, HPV, and more.
- **Screenings**: Mammograms, colonoscopies, cholesterol tests, and diabetes screenings.

How to Use Preventive Services

- **Schedule Regular Appointments**: Make sure to schedule your annual physical and any recommended screenings.
- **Know What's Covered**: Review your insurance policy to understand which preventive services are covered at no cost to you.
- **Stay Informed**: Keep up-to-date with the recommended preventive services for your age and health condition.

Using In-Network Providers

Using in-network providers is crucial for minimizing your healthcare costs. In-network providers have contracted with your insurance company to offer services at discounted rates.

Benefits of In-Network Providers

- **Lower Costs**: Services from in-network providers typically cost less than those from out-of-network providers.
- **Simplified Billing**: In-network providers handle billing directly with your insurance company, reducing the hassle for you.
- **Coordinated Care**: In-network providers often work together, ensuring better coordination of your care.

Finding In-Network Providers

- **Insurance Company Website**: Most insurance companies have online directories where you can search for in-network providers.
- **Customer Service**: Call your insurance company's customer service for assistance in finding in-network providers.
- **Provider's Office**: Verify with your provider's office that they are in-network before scheduling an appointment.

Understanding and Using Telehealth

Telehealth has become an increasingly popular option for accessing healthcare services. It offers convenience and often lower costs compared to in-person visits.

Benefits of Telehealth

- **Convenience**: Access healthcare from the comfort of your home, reducing the need for travel and time off work.
- **Lower Costs**: Telehealth visits are often less expensive than

in-person visits.
- **Access to Specialists**: Telehealth can provide access to specialists who may not be available locally.

Examples of Telehealth Services

- **Virtual Doctor Visits**: Consult with your primary care physician or specialist via video call.
- **Mental Health Services**: Access therapy and counseling sessions online.
- **Remote Monitoring**: Use digital tools to monitor chronic conditions and share data with your healthcare provider.

How to Use Telehealth

- **Check Coverage**: Confirm that telehealth services are covered by your insurance plan.
- **Choose a Platform**: Use your insurance company's preferred telehealth platform or a reputable telehealth service.
- **Schedule an Appointment**: Schedule a telehealth appointment just as you would for an in-person visit.

Managing Medications

Properly managing your medications can lead to significant cost savings and better health outcomes.

Understanding Your Plan's Formulary

- **Formulary**: A list of medications covered by your insurance plan. It categorizes drugs into tiers, each with different cost levels.
- **Tiers**: Medications in lower tiers generally cost less. Understanding which tier your medication falls into can help you manage costs.

Cost-Saving Strategies for Medications

- **Generic Drugs**: Opt for generic versions of brand-name drugs whenever possible. They are equally effective and typically much cheaper.
- **Mail-Order Pharmacies**: Many insurance plans offer mail-order pharmacy services that provide medications at a lower cost and greater convenience.
- **90-Day Supplies**: If you take medications regularly, getting a 90-day supply can reduce costs and the frequency of refills.

Examples of Managing Medications

- **Jane's Asthma Management**: Jane uses a mail-order pharmacy to get a 90-day supply of her asthma medication, saving money and ensuring she never runs out.
- **Tom's High Blood Pressure**: Tom switches to a generic version of his high blood pressure medication, cutting his monthly medication costs by half.

Understanding Additional Plan Features

Health insurance plans often come with additional features that can enhance your benefits and save you money.

Wellness Programs

Many insurance plans offer wellness programs aimed at promoting healthy lifestyles and preventing illness. These programs may include:

- **Fitness Discounts**: Discounts on gym memberships or fitness classes.
- **Smoking Cessation Programs**: Support and resources to help you quit smoking.
- **Weight Loss Programs**: Access to weight loss programs and counseling.

Employee Assistance Programs (EAPs)

EAPs provide a range of services to support your mental and emotional well-being, including:

- **Counseling Services**: Confidential counseling for personal or work-related issues.
- **Financial Planning**: Assistance with financial planning and debt management.
- **Legal Services**: Access to legal advice and services.

Health Coaching

Some plans offer health coaching services, where you can work with a health coach to set and achieve health goals. These services might include:

- **Personalized Health Plans**: Developing a customized health plan based on your needs and goals.
- **Regular Check-Ins**: Ongoing support and motivation to help you stay on track.

Examples of Additional Plan Features

- **Emma's Wellness Program**: Emma's insurance plan includes a wellness program that offers a discount on her gym membership. She takes advantage of this benefit to stay active and healthy.
- **Mark's EAP**: Mark uses his Employee Assistance Program to get counseling services during a stressful period at work. The support helps him manage his stress and maintain his mental health.

Useful Websites

- GoodRx: Compare prescription drug prices and find discounts.
- Telehealth.HHS.gov: Information on telehealth services and how to use them.
- CDC Preventive Services: Information on recommended preventive services.
- Wellness Programs: Resources and information on various

wellness programs.

By maximizing your health insurance benefits through preventive care, using in-network providers, leveraging telehealth, managing medications effectively, and taking advantage of additional plan features, you can significantly reduce your healthcare costs and improve your overall health. These strategies will help you get the most out of your health insurance and support your journey toward financial stability.

Chapter 4: Financial Strategies for Health Insurance

Health insurance is not just about protecting your health; it can also be a crucial component of your financial strategy. This chapter will explore various financial strategies, including Health Savings Accounts (HSAs), Flexible Spending Accounts (FSAs), tax deductions and credits, and other ways to maximize the financial benefits of your health insurance.

Health Savings Accounts (HSAs)

An HSA is a tax-advantaged account designed to help individuals save for medical expenses. It is available to those enrolled in high-deductible health plans (HDHPs).

Benefits of HSAs

- **Tax Advantages**: Contributions to an HSA are tax-deductible, reducing your taxable income. The money in your HSA grows tax-free, and withdrawals for qualified medical expenses are also tax-free.
- **Flexibility**: HSAs can be used for a wide range of qualified medical expenses, including deductibles, copayments, coin-

surance, and some over-the-counter medications.
- **Rollover**: Unlike FSAs, unused HSA funds roll over year to year, allowing you to build a substantial balance over time.
- **Portability**: HSAs are owned by the individual, not the employer, so the account stays with you even if you change jobs.

How to Use an HSA

1. **Open an HSA**: You can open an HSA through many banks, credit unions, or insurance companies.
2. **Contribute Regularly**: Contribute up to the annual limit set by the IRS. For 2024, the limits are $3,650 for individuals and $7,300 for families.
3. **Invest Your Funds**: Many HSA providers offer investment options, allowing you to grow your savings over time.
4. **Track Expenses**: Keep receipts and records of your medical expenses for tax purposes.

Example

Emma, a self-employed graphic designer, opens an HSA with her HDHP. She contributes the maximum amount each year, reducing her taxable income. She uses the HSA to pay for medical expenses, such as doctor visits and prescriptions, and invests the remaining funds for future use.

Flexible Spending Accounts (FSAs)

FSAs are employer-sponsored accounts that allow you to set aside pre-tax dollars for eligible medical expenses. FSAs have different rules compared to HSAs.

Benefits of FSAs

- **Tax Savings**: Contributions to an FSA reduce your taxable income.
- **Immediate Availability**: The total amount you elect to contribute is available at the beginning of the plan year, even if you haven't fully funded the account yet.

Limitations of FSAs

- **Use-It-Or-Lose-It**: Unused funds typically do not roll over to the next year, although some plans offer a grace period or a limited rollover amount.
- **Employer Control**: FSAs are tied to your employer, so you may lose the funds if you change jobs.

How to Use an FSA

1. **Enroll During Open Enrollment**: Choose the amount you want to contribute for the year.
2. **Submit Claims**: Use your FSA funds for eligible expenses and submit claims for reimbursement.
3. **Plan Your Spending**: Estimate your medical expenses carefully to avoid losing unused funds at the end of the year.

Example

John, an employee at a marketing firm, enrolls in his employer's FSA during open enrollment. He contributes $2,500 for the year, which he uses for his family's medical expenses, including dental work and prescription glasses.

Tax Deductions and Credits

Tax deductions and credits related to health insurance can provide significant savings, especially for self-employed individuals and those with high medical expenses.

Self-Employed Health Insurance Deduction

Self-employed individuals can deduct the cost of health insurance premiums for themselves, their spouse, and dependents. This deduction is available even if you do not itemize deductions on your tax return.

Itemized Deductions for Medical Expenses

If you itemize deductions on your tax return, you can deduct medical expenses that exceed 7.5% of your adjusted gross income (AGI). Eligible expenses include:

- **Premiums**: For health insurance and long-term care insurance.
- **Out-of-Pocket Costs**: For medical, dental, and vision care.
- **Transportation**: Costs for traveling to medical appointments.

Health Coverage Tax Credit (HCTC)

The HCTC is available to certain individuals who qualify for specific trade adjustment assistance programs or are receiving pension payments from the Pension Benefit Guaranty Corporation. It covers a significant portion of your health insurance premiums.

Example

Lisa, a freelance writer, deducts her health insurance premiums on her tax return, reducing her taxable income. She also itemizes her deductions and includes her out-of-pocket medical expenses, which exceed 7.5% of her AGI, further lowering her tax bill.

Reducing Healthcare Costs Through Financial Strategies

Maximizing your health insurance benefits and strategically managing your healthcare expenses can lead to substantial savings.

Shopping for Services

- **Price Transparency Tools**: Use online tools to compare prices for medical services and procedures. Websites like Healthcare Bluebook and Fair Health Consumer can help you find the best prices.
- **Negotiating Medical Bills**: Don't be afraid to negotiate with healthcare providers and hospitals. Many are willing to reduce bills if you ask.

Using Preventive Services

Preventive care is often covered at no additional cost under most health insurance plans. Utilizing these services can help you avoid more costly treatments in the future.

Example

Mark uses an online price transparency tool to compare prices for a knee surgery. He chooses a provider that offers the surgery at a lower cost, saving him several thousand dollars. After the surgery, he negotiates his medical bills, further reducing his expenses.

Utilizing Employer Benefits

Many employers offer additional benefits that can help reduce healthcare costs and improve financial stability.

Wellness Programs

- **Fitness Discounts**: Discounts on gym memberships or fitness classes.
- **Smoking Cessation Programs**: Support and resources to help you quit smoking.
- **Weight Loss Programs**: Access to weight loss programs and counseling.

Employee Assistance Programs (EAPs)

EAPs provide a range of services to support your mental and emotional well-being, including:

- **Counseling Services**: Confidential counseling for personal or work-related issues.
- **Financial Planning**: Assistance with financial planning and debt management.
- **Legal Services**: Access to legal advice and services.

Example

Sarah's employer offers a comprehensive wellness program that includes a discount on her gym membership and access to a weight loss program. She takes advantage of these benefits to improve her health and save money on fitness expenses.

Useful Websites

- IRS HSA Information: Details on HSAs and other tax-advantaged health accounts.
- FSA Store: A resource for eligible FSA expenses and products.
- Healthcare Bluebook: Compare prices for medical procedures.
- Fair Health Consumer: Estimates for medical and dental procedures.
- HHS.gov: Information on healthcare rights and the ACA.
- Department of Labor COBRA Information: Details on COBRA coverage.

By leveraging financial strategies such as HSAs, FSAs, tax deductions, and employer benefits, you can maximize the financial benefits of your health insurance. These strategies can help you save money, reduce your tax burden, and ensure that you are financially prepared for healthcare expenses.

Chapter 5: Reducing Healthcare Costs

Reducing healthcare costs is essential for achieving financial stability. This chapter will provide practical strategies for shopping for services, negotiating medical bills, understanding medical billing errors, and utilizing cost-saving resources.

Shopping for Services

Healthcare costs can vary widely between providers and facilities. Shopping for services can help you find the best prices for the care you need.

Price Transparency Tools

Price transparency tools can help you compare costs for medical services and procedures. These tools provide information on the average costs in your area, allowing you to make informed decisions about where to receive care.

- **Healthcare Bluebook**: Offers price comparisons for medical procedures and services.
- **Fair Health Consumer**: Provides cost estimates for medical and dental procedures based on your location.

- **GoodRx**: Compares prescription drug prices and provides discounts.

Example

Jessica needs a knee replacement surgery. She uses Healthcare Bluebook to compare prices at different hospitals in her area. By choosing a hospital with lower costs, she saves several thousand dollars on the procedure.

Negotiating Medical Bills

Medical bills can be overwhelming, but negotiating with healthcare providers can lead to significant savings. Many providers are willing to work with patients to reduce their bills, set up payment plans, or offer financial assistance.

Steps to Negotiate Medical Bills

1. **Review Your Bill**: Carefully review your medical bill for accuracy. Look for any errors or charges for services you did not receive.
2. **Understand Your Insurance Coverage**: Know what your insurance covers and what you are responsible for paying out-of-pocket.
3. **Contact the Provider**: Call the billing department of the healthcare provider to discuss your bill. Be polite and explain your situation.
4. **Ask for a Discount**: Request a discount or financial assistance. Many providers have programs to help patients with high medical bills.

5. **Set Up a Payment Plan**: If you cannot pay the bill in full, ask about setting up a payment plan with manageable monthly payments.

Example

David receives a $5,000 bill for an emergency room visit. After reviewing the bill, he notices charges for services he did not receive. He contacts the hospital's billing department, corrects the errors, and negotiates a 20% discount on the remaining balance. He also sets up a payment plan to pay off the bill over six months.

Understanding Medical Billing Errors

Medical billing errors are common and can lead to inflated healthcare costs. Understanding how to identify and address these errors can save you money.

Common Medical Billing Errors

- **Duplicate Charges**: Being charged twice for the same service.
- **Incorrect Coding**: Errors in the medical codes used to bill for services.
- **Unnecessary Services**: Charges for services you did not receive or that were not medically necessary.
- **Insurance Processing Errors**: Mistakes in how your insurance processed the claim.

Steps to Address Billing Errors

1. **Request an Itemized Bill**: Ask for an itemized bill that details each charge.
2. **Compare with Explanation of Benefits (EOB)**: Review your insurance company's Explanation of Benefits (EOB) to see what was covered and what you owe.
3. **Highlight Errors**: Highlight any discrepancies or charges you do not understand.
4. **Contact the Provider**: Call the billing department to discuss and correct the errors.
5. **Follow Up**: Keep records of your communications and follow up until the issue is resolved.

Example

Emily receives a bill for her recent hospital stay and notices a charge for an MRI she did not have. She requests an itemized bill, compares it with her EOB, and contacts the hospital to correct the error, reducing her bill by $1,200.

Utilizing Cost-Saving Resources

There are various resources available to help you reduce healthcare costs. These resources can provide discounts, financial assistance, and information on low-cost services.

Prescription Discount Programs

- **GoodRx**: Offers discounts on prescription medications at participating pharmacies.
- **SingleCare**: Provides discount cards for prescription medications.
- **NeedyMeds**: Connects patients with assistance programs for medications and healthcare services.

Community Health Clinics

- **Federally Qualified Health Centers (FQHCs)**: Provide low-cost or sliding-scale fee services based on your income.
- **Free Clinics**: Offer free healthcare services to uninsured and underinsured individuals.
- **State and Local Health Departments**: May provide low-cost or free services, including vaccinations and screenings.

Financial Assistance Programs

- **Hospital Financial Assistance Programs**: Many hospitals offer financial assistance to patients with low incomes or high medical bills.
- **Nonprofit Organizations**: Organizations like the Patient Advocate Foundation and HealthWell Foundation offer financial assistance for medical expenses.

Examples of Cost-Saving Resources

Example 1: Prescription Discount Program

Sarah needs a prescription medication that is not covered by her insurance. She uses GoodRx to find a coupon that reduces the cost of her medication from $150 to $40 at a local pharmacy.

Example 2: Community Health Clinic

Mike, who is uninsured, visits a Federally Qualified Health Center (FQHC) for his annual check-up. He pays a sliding-scale fee based on his income, making the visit affordable at $20.

Example 3: Financial Assistance Program

Laura faces a $10,000 bill for her cancer treatment. She applies for financial assistance through the hospital's charity care program and qualifies for a 50% reduction in her bill. She also receives a grant from the HealthWell Foundation to cover additional costs.

Useful Websites

- Healthcare Bluebook: Compare prices for medical procedures.
- Fair Health Consumer: Estimates for medical and dental procedures.
- GoodRx: Compare prescription drug prices and find discounts.
- SingleCare: Prescription discount cards.
- NeedyMeds: Assistance programs for medications and healthcare services.

- HRSA Health Center Finder: Locate Federally Qualified Health Centers.
- Patient Advocate Foundation: Financial assistance for medical expenses.
- HealthWell Foundation: Grants for medical expenses.

By shopping for services, negotiating medical bills, understanding and correcting billing errors, and utilizing cost-saving resources, you can significantly reduce your healthcare costs. These strategies will help you manage your healthcare expenses more effectively, contributing to your overall financial stability.

Chapter 6: Legal Considerations

Understanding your legal rights and responsibilities regarding health insurance can help you navigate the healthcare system more effectively and avoid unnecessary costs. This chapter will cover essential legal aspects, including knowing your rights under the Affordable Care Act (ACA), the process for appealing denied claims, filing grievances, understanding COBRA, and other important legal protections.

Knowing Your Rights Under the Affordable Care Act (ACA)

The ACA, also known as Obamacare, introduced several key protections and benefits for health insurance consumers. Being aware of these rights can help you make informed decisions and ensure you receive the coverage you are entitled to.

Key Provisions of the ACA

- **Pre-Existing Conditions**: Insurers cannot deny coverage or charge higher premiums based on pre-existing conditions.
- **Essential Health Benefits**: All ACA-compliant plans must cover a set of essential health benefits, including hospitalization, maternity care, mental health services, and

prescription drugs.
- **Preventive Services**: Preventive services, such as screenings and vaccinations, must be covered without cost-sharing.
- **Dependent Coverage**: You can keep your children on your health insurance plan until they turn 26.
- **No Lifetime Limits**: The ACA prohibits lifetime limits on essential health benefits.
- **Out-of-Pocket Maximums**: There are limits on how much you can be required to pay out-of-pocket each year for covered services.

Example

Karen has diabetes, a pre-existing condition. Thanks to the ACA, she cannot be denied health insurance coverage or charged higher premiums because of her condition. Her ACA-compliant plan also covers her insulin and regular check-ups without imposing lifetime limits on her benefits.

Appeals and Grievances

If your health insurance claim is denied or you have a complaint about your coverage, you have the right to appeal and file a grievance. Understanding this process can help you resolve issues and ensure you receive the benefits you are entitled to.

Steps to Appeal a Denied Claim

1. **Review the Denial**: Carefully read the denial letter from your insurer to understand the reason for the denial.
2. **Gather Information**: Collect all relevant information, including medical records, doctor's notes, and any correspondence with your insurer.
3. **Submit an Internal Appeal**: Write a formal appeal letter to your insurance company explaining why the denial should be reversed. Include supporting documentation.
4. **Request an External Review**: If the internal appeal is denied, you can request an independent external review. An external reviewer will evaluate your case and make a binding decision.

Example

John's insurance company denies his claim for a necessary surgery, stating it is not medically necessary. John reviews the denial letter and gathers supporting documentation from his doctor. He submits an internal appeal, including a letter from his doctor explaining the medical necessity of the surgery. When the internal appeal is denied, John requests an external review. The external reviewer overturns the denial, and John's surgery is approved.

Filing Grievances

If you have a complaint about your health insurance plan, such as issues with customer service, coverage decisions, or access to care, you can file a grievance with your insurer.

Steps to File a Grievance

1. **Contact Your Insurer**: Begin by contacting your insurer's customer service department to try to resolve the issue informally.
2. **Submit a Formal Grievance**: If the issue is not resolved, submit a formal grievance in writing. Include details about the problem and any supporting documentation.
3. **Follow Up**: Keep records of your communications and follow up with your insurer to ensure your grievance is addressed.

Example

Maria experiences repeated delays in getting approval for her physical therapy sessions. She contacts her insurer's customer service but receives no resolution. She then files a formal grievance, detailing the delays and their impact on her health. The insurer reviews her grievance and resolves the issue, ensuring her therapy sessions are approved promptly.

Understanding COBRA

The Consolidated Omnibus Budget Reconciliation Act (COBRA) allows you to continue your employer-sponsored health insurance coverage for a limited time after losing your job or experiencing another qualifying event. COBRA can provide a critical safety net during transitions.

Key Aspects of COBRA

- **Eligibility**: COBRA is available if you lose your job (voluntarily or involuntarily), have reduced work hours, or experience another qualifying event such as divorce or death of the covered employee.
- **Coverage Period**: COBRA coverage generally lasts up to 18 months but can be extended to 36 months in certain situations.
- **Cost**: You are responsible for paying the full premium, including the portion previously paid by your employer, plus a 2% administrative fee.

How to Enroll in COBRA

1. **Receive Notification**: Your employer must provide you with a COBRA election notice within 14 days of your qualifying event.
2. **Elect Coverage**: You have 60 days from the date of the notice to elect COBRA coverage.
3. **Pay Premiums**: Pay the required premiums to maintain coverage.

Example

After being laid off from her job, Linda receives a COBRA election notice. She elects COBRA coverage within the 60-day window and pays the full premium to continue her health insurance while she looks for a new job.

CHAPTER 6: LEGAL CONSIDERATIONS

Legal Protections for Health Insurance Consumers

Beyond the ACA and COBRA, several other laws and regulations protect health insurance consumers. Understanding these protections can help you navigate the healthcare system more effectively.

Health Insurance Portability and Accountability Act (HIPAA)

- **Privacy Protections**: HIPAA protects the privacy of your health information and sets standards for how it can be used and disclosed.
- **Portability Protections**: HIPAA ensures that you can obtain health insurance even if you have pre-existing conditions, provided you have maintained continuous coverage.

Mental Health Parity and Addiction Equity Act (MHPAEA)

- **Parity Protections**: MHPAEA requires that health insurance plans offering mental health and substance use disorder benefits provide them at parity with medical and surgical benefits. This means that financial requirements (like copayments and deductibles) and treatment limits (like visit limits) for mental health and substance use disorder services cannot be more restrictive than those for medical and surgical services.

Example

Michael, who has been receiving mental health treatment, finds that his insurance is charging higher copayments for mental health visits compared to medical visits. He files a complaint with his insurer, citing the MHPAEA, and the insurer adjusts the copayments to ensure parity.

Useful Websites

- Healthcare.gov: Information on the ACA and health insurance marketplaces.
- Department of Labor: Information on COBRA, health plan rights, and other employee benefits.
- HHS.gov: Information on HIPAA, patient rights, and healthcare regulations.
- CMS.gov: Information on Medicare, Medicaid, and CHIP.
- Parity Implementation Coalition: Information and resources on mental health parity.

By understanding your legal rights and responsibilities regarding health insurance, you can better navigate the healthcare system, protect yourself from unnecessary costs, and ensure you receive the benefits you are entitled to. These legal considerations are essential for maintaining both your health and financial stability.

CHAPTER 6: LEGAL CONSIDERATIONS

Chapter 7: Long-Term Planning and Health Insurance

Long-term planning for health insurance involves understanding how your coverage needs may change over time and ensuring you have adequate protection for future healthcare expenses. This chapter will explore health insurance considerations for retirement, long-term care insurance, and estate planning, providing strategies to help you prepare for the future.

Insurance and Retirement

As you approach retirement, your health insurance needs will change. It's crucial to understand the options available to you and how to integrate them into your overall retirement plan.

Medicare

Medicare is a federal health insurance program for people aged 65 and older, and for some younger people with disabilities. It consists of several parts, each covering different aspects of healthcare.

- **Medicare Part A**: Covers hospital stays, skilled nursing

facility care, hospice care, and some home health care. Most people do not pay a premium for Part A if they or their spouse paid Medicare taxes while working.
- **Medicare Part B**: Covers outpatient care, preventive services, ambulance services, and medical equipment. Part B requires a monthly premium.
- **Medicare Part C (Medicare Advantage)**: An alternative to Original Medicare (Parts A and B), offered by private insurance companies approved by Medicare. These plans often include Part D (prescription drug coverage) and may offer additional benefits.
- **Medicare Part D**: Provides prescription drug coverage. You can join a Part D plan if you have Part A or Part B.

Medigap (Medicare Supplement Insurance)

Medigap policies are sold by private companies and can help pay some of the healthcare costs that Original Medicare does not cover, such as copayments, coinsurance, and deductibles. There are different Medigap plans, each offering different levels of coverage.

Retirement Health Insurance Strategies

1. **Evaluate Your Needs**: Consider your current health status and any chronic conditions that may require ongoing treatment.
2. **Enroll in Medicare**: Sign up for Medicare during your Initial Enrollment Period (IEP), which begins three months before you turn 65 and ends three months after your 65th birthday.

3. **Consider a Medigap Policy**: If you have Original Medicare, evaluate whether a Medigap policy would help cover additional costs.
4. **Explore Medicare Advantage**: Compare Medicare Advantage plans to see if they offer benefits that meet your needs, such as vision, dental, or hearing coverage.
5. **Review Prescription Drug Coverage**: Ensure you have adequate prescription drug coverage through a Part D plan or a Medicare Advantage plan that includes drug coverage.

Example

Alice, approaching her 65th birthday, starts researching Medicare options. She decides to enroll in Medicare Part A and Part B and also chooses a Medigap Plan G to cover additional expenses. She adds a Part D plan to cover her prescription medications, ensuring comprehensive coverage in retirement.

Planning for Long-Term Care

Long-term care insurance covers services not typically included in standard health insurance, such as assistance with daily activities, home care, assisted living, and nursing home care. Planning for long-term care is essential as you age, given the high costs associated with these services.

Long-Term Care Insurance

- **Coverage**: Long-term care insurance can help cover the costs of long-term care services, including personal and custodial care in various settings such as your home, a

community organization, or other facilities.
- **Eligibility**: Generally, you must be in good health to purchase a long-term care insurance policy. Premiums are based on your age and health at the time of purchase.
- **Benefits**: Policies vary, but benefits often include a daily or monthly benefit amount, a benefit period, and an elimination period (waiting period before benefits begin).

Self-Funding Long-Term Care

If you choose not to purchase long-term care insurance, you need a plan to self-fund potential long-term care expenses. This may involve:

- **Savings**: Building a dedicated savings account or investment portfolio for long-term care costs.
- **Home Equity**: Using the equity in your home through a reverse mortgage or selling your home to fund long-term care.
- **Life Insurance**: Some life insurance policies offer long-term care riders, allowing you to access a portion of the death benefit to cover long-term care expenses.

Example

Bob and Susan, both in their early 60s, purchase long-term care insurance policies to cover potential future needs. Their policies provide a daily benefit of $200 with a benefit period of three years. This coverage ensures they have financial support for home care or nursing home care if needed.

Estate Planning and Health Insurance

Estate planning involves preparing for the transfer of your assets after your death and managing your affairs if you become incapacitated. Integrating health insurance considerations into your estate plan can ensure your healthcare wishes are followed and your financial resources are protected.

Health Care Directives

- **Living Will**: A document that outlines your wishes for medical treatment if you become unable to communicate them yourself.
- **Durable Power of Attorney for Health Care**: Designates someone to make healthcare decisions on your behalf if you are incapacitated.

Financial Power of Attorney

A financial power of attorney designates someone to manage your financial affairs, including health insurance matters, if you are unable to do so yourself.

Trusts

- **Revocable Living Trust**: Can include provisions for managing your assets and health insurance needs if you become incapacitated. It can also facilitate the transfer of assets upon your death without going through probate.
- **Irrevocable Trust**: Can protect assets from being depleted by long-term care costs, potentially allowing you to qualify

for Medicaid.

Example

Michael and Linda create an estate plan that includes a living will and durable power of attorney for health care. They also establish a revocable living trust to manage their assets and ensure their healthcare and financial wishes are followed if they become incapacitated.

Resources for Long-Term Planning

- **Medicare.gov**: Comprehensive information on Medicare plans, enrollment, and benefits.
- **LongTermCare.gov**: Resources and information on planning for long-term care, including costs and options.
- **AARP Medicare**: Information and resources on Medicare options and supplemental insurance.
- **Eldercare Locator**: A public service of the U.S. Administration on Aging connecting you to services for older adults and their families.
- **National Association of Insurance Commissioners (NAIC)**: Guides and resources for long-term care insurance and other health insurance options.
- **LegalZoom**: Online estate planning tools and resources.

By understanding health insurance options for retirement, planning for long-term care, and incorporating health insurance considerations into your estate plan, you can ensure you are financially and medically prepared for the future. These strategies will help you maintain your financial stability and peace of mind as you age.

Chapter 8: Leveraging Technology for Health Insurance Management

In today's digital age, technology plays a crucial role in managing your health insurance and overall healthcare. This chapter explores various technological tools and resources that can help you stay organized, informed, and proactive about your health insurance and medical care.

Health Insurance Portals and Mobile Apps

Most health insurance providers offer online portals and mobile apps that provide easy access to your health insurance information. These tools can help you manage your plan, track claims, and stay informed about your coverage.

Features of Health Insurance Portals and Apps

- **Plan Details**: Access information about your plan, including coverage details, deductibles, copayments, and out-of-pocket maximums.
- **Claims Tracking**: View the status of your claims, including what has been paid and what you owe.
- **Provider Search**: Find in-network doctors, hospitals, and

specialists.
- **ID Cards**: Access digital copies of your insurance ID card.
- **Cost Estimators**: Estimate the costs of medical procedures and services.
- **Telehealth Access**: Connect to telehealth services for virtual consultations.

Example

Sarah uses her health insurance provider's mobile app to check her coverage details and track the status of her recent claims. She also uses the app to find an in-network specialist for her upcoming appointment, saving time and ensuring she gets the most out of her coverage.

Personal Health Records (PHRs)

Personal Health Records (PHRs) are electronic applications that allow you to maintain and manage your health information in a secure and private environment. PHRs can be helpful in organizing your medical history, tracking medications, and sharing information with healthcare providers.

Benefits of PHRs

- **Comprehensive Records**: Keep all your medical information in one place, including doctor visits, test results, medications, and immunizations.
- **Accessibility**: Access your health records from anywhere, at any time.
- **Coordination of Care**: Share your PHR with multiple health-

CHAPTER 8: LEVERAGING TECHNOLOGY FOR HEALTH INSURANCE...

care providers to ensure coordinated and informed care.

Popular PHR Platforms

- **MyChart**: Offered by many healthcare systems, MyChart allows patients to access their medical records, schedule appointments, and communicate with their healthcare providers.
- **Microsoft HealthVault**: A platform that lets you store and manage your health information securely.
- **Apple Health**: Integrates health data from various sources, including medical records, wearable devices, and third-party apps.

Example

John uses MyChart to keep track of his medical history and appointments. When he visits a new specialist, he shares his PHR to provide a complete picture of his health, ensuring the specialist has all the necessary information for an accurate diagnosis and treatment plan.

Telehealth and Virtual Care

Telehealth services have become increasingly popular, providing convenient and cost-effective access to healthcare. Telehealth can be used for a variety of medical needs, from routine consultations to mental health services.

Advantages of Telehealth

- **Convenience**: Access healthcare from the comfort of your home, reducing the need for travel and time off work.
- **Cost Savings**: Telehealth visits are often less expensive than in-person visits.
- **Access to Specialists**: Consult with specialists who may not be available locally.

Types of Telehealth Services

- **Virtual Doctor Visits**: Consult with your primary care physician or specialist via video call.
- **Mental Health Services**: Access therapy and counseling sessions online.
- **Remote Monitoring**: Use digital tools to monitor chronic conditions and share data with your healthcare provider.

Example

Emma uses telehealth services to manage her anxiety. She has regular video sessions with her therapist, which are covered by her insurance plan. The convenience of telehealth allows her to maintain consistent care without the stress of traveling to appointments.

Health and Fitness Apps

Health and fitness apps can help you maintain a healthy lifestyle, track your progress, and manage chronic conditions. Many apps integrate with wearable devices to provide real-time data and insights.

Popular Health and Fitness Apps

- **MyFitnessPal**: A comprehensive app for tracking diet and exercise.
- **Fitbit**: Tracks physical activity, sleep, and heart rate, and provides insights to improve your health.
- **Headspace**: Offers guided meditation and mindfulness exercises to support mental well-being.

Integrating Apps with Health Insurance

Some health insurance plans offer incentives for using health and fitness apps. These incentives may include discounts on premiums, rewards for meeting health goals, and access to wellness programs.

Example

Tom uses a combination of MyFitnessPal and Fitbit to track his diet and exercise. His health insurance plan offers a discount on his premiums for meeting certain activity goals, providing an extra incentive to stay active and healthy.

Wearable Technology

Wearable devices, such as fitness trackers and smartwatches, can provide valuable health data and help you stay on top of your fitness goals. These devices can monitor physical activity, heart rate, sleep patterns, and more.

Benefits of Wearable Technology

- **Real-Time Monitoring**: Get immediate feedback on your health metrics.
- **Goal Setting**: Set and track fitness goals, such as steps taken, calories burned, and active minutes.
- **Health Alerts**: Receive alerts for irregular heart rates, reminders to move, and notifications to take medications.

Example

Linda wears a smartwatch that tracks her physical activity and monitors her heart rate. The data syncs with her health insurance app, which offers rewards for meeting her daily step goals and maintaining a healthy heart rate.

Online Health Communities

Online health communities provide a platform for individuals to share experiences, seek advice, and find support for various health conditions. These communities can be a valuable resource for information and emotional support.

Benefits of Online Health Communities

- **Peer Support**: Connect with others who have similar health conditions and share experiences.
- **Information Sharing**: Access a wealth of information from people who have firsthand experience with treatments, medications, and healthcare providers.
- **Emotional Support**: Find encouragement and understand-

ing from a supportive community.

Popular Online Health Communities

- **PatientsLikeMe**: A platform where patients can share their health data and experiences to help others.
- **Inspire**: Connects patients, caregivers, and health professionals for support and information sharing.
- **HealthUnlocked**: A social network for health, providing forums for various health conditions.

Example

Karen joins an online community for people with rheumatoid arthritis. She connects with others who share their experiences with different treatments and provides emotional support. The information and encouragement she receives help her manage her condition more effectively.

Useful Websites and Apps

- **MyChart**: mychart.com
- **Microsoft HealthVault**: healthvault.com
- **Apple Health**: apple.com/health
- **GoodRx**: goodrx.com
- **MyFitnessPal**: myfitnesspal.com
- **Fitbit**: fitbit.com
- **Headspace**: headspace.com
- **PatientsLikeMe**: patientslikeme.com
- **Inspire**: inspire.com
- **HealthUnlocked**: healthunlocked.com

Leveraging technology for health insurance management can help you stay organized, informed, and proactive about your healthcare. By using health insurance portals and apps, maintaining personal health records, utilizing telehealth services, and engaging with health and fitness apps and online communities, you can enhance your health insurance experience and improve your overall health and well-being.

Conclusion

Conclusion

Health insurance is a powerful tool in achieving financial stability. By understanding and maximizing your health insurance benefits, you can significantly reduce your healthcare costs and protect yourself from financial hardship due to medical expenses. Use this knowledge to make informed decisions and integrate health insurance into your broader financial strategy.

Resources

- Healthcare.gov: Official health insurance marketplace
- IRS.gov: Information on HSAs and FSAs
- Medicare.gov: Official Medicare information and resources

www.ingramcontent.com/pod-product-compliance
Lightning Source LLC
Chambersburg PA
CBHW071843210526
45479CB00001B/260